A is for Ailm
(pronounced 'A-lum')

Predominantly associated with Elm, but also Pine and Fir, these tall straight trees are the embodiment of perspective and height. In ancient Celtic tree lore, the Elm is intimately bound up with death and the transition into the Underworld, whilst evergreen Fir trees were associated with the healing of a person's soul.

The kind of elm that grows most widely in Scotland is Wych Elm. This refers not to witches, who were said to shun Elm trees, but refers to its flexibility, taken from an Old English verb meaning 'to give way'. As wood from the Elm is very flexible it does not make a good material to construct buildings from. However, like Alder it does withstand water very well, so it has been popular in making boat hulls, bridges and wheels. Like Scots Pine, hollowed out Elm has previously been used as water piping before the advent of metal water pipes. Elm is also the material that coffins were traditionally made from. Welsh longbows were often made from Elm, whereas English longbows were usually Yew.

Beith

B is for Beith
(pronounced 'BAE-yh')

Beith is is associated with Birch (particularly Silver Birch). Known as 'The Lady of the Woods', in Celtic mythology Birch represents purification, change and new beginnings, femininity, grace, purity, family connections, protection, healing, new life and rebirth.

As Birch is one of the first trees to come into leaf it would be an obvious choice as a representation of the emergence of Spring. The Birch is known as a 'Pioneer Tree' meaning that it can restart the colonisation of woodlands after long-term natural disasters. According to Highland folklore, a barren cow herded with a Birch stick would become fertile

Birch bark was used for tanning leather whilst Birch wood is tough, heavy and straight-grained, and was historically used to make infants cradles, cabinets and furniture. It is also used to make besom brooms, the archetypal witches' broomsticks upon which they were said to fly (maybe due to the consumption of Fly Agaric mushrooms that typically grow beneath Birch trees in Autumn).

C is for Coll
(pronounced 'Col')

Coll is associated with Hazel. In Celtic mythology Hazel is associated with wisdom, creativity and knowledge. The Hazel is one of the oldest native British trees. Traces of hazelnut shells and pollen have been discovered in cave settlements dating back around 10,000 years.

Pliable, straight shoots called 'withies' grow up from the base of the Hazel and these are still cut for walking sticks and pinned into shape whilst growing, for shepherd's crooks. Pilgrims often used to make staffs from Hazel, providing a sturdy walking stick and a means of self-defence. Hazel was used in the weaving of baskets in medieval times.

August is known as the Hazel Moon as this is when Hazel nuts appear on the trees. The red spots on wild salmon were reputedly gained when the fish consumed nine hazelnuts that fell into a pool from a surrounding grove.

D is for Dair
(pronounced 'Dahr')

Dair is associated with Oak. In Celtic lore and mythology the Oak is associated with strength, resilience and self-confidence. It is a great tree for enhancing inner strength, especially when you have experienced a loss in life. It is said that the Oak tree helps lend power so you might rebuild your life and move forward.

Oak has been valued for its strength and durability. It was commonly used in the construction of homes and the bark has been used in the tanning industry.

St. Columba was said to have had a fondness and respect for Oak trees, and to have been reluctant to fell them, although his early chapel on Iona was constructed of Oak from the nearby Mull Oakwoods.

E is for Eadha
(pronounced 'EH-ga')

Eadha is associated with Aspen. Aspen is seen as a symbol of endurance, courage and the overcoming of obstacles. In the Scottish Highlands, the Aspen was often rumoured to be connected to the realm of the faeries.

There was a Highland tradition of not using wood from the Aspen for fishing, agricultural implements or in house construction, suggesting that the Aspen was considered a faerie tree on a par with the Rowan tree, the use of whose wood holds similar taboos.

However, Aspen wood is very lightweight and when dried, becomes very buoyant, and was therefore historically a popular choice for oars and paddles. Weight for weight it also offers unrivalled protection and was the wood of choice for shields and armour. In Celtic mythology, Aspen was also seen as providing spiritual protection as well. The unique shape of the leaves creates a whispering sound in a breeze, which the Celts believed was the souls of their ancestors communicating.

F is for Feàrn
(pronounced 'Fyaarn')

Feàrn is associated with Alder. In Celtic Mythology, Alder is often associated with water, secrecy, nature, bad luck, spirituality, and balance. Alder trees were also a source of great mystery to the Celts as their sap turns a deep red when exposed to the air, as if they could bleed when cut.

In Irish mythology Deirdre of the Sorrows fled to Alba (Scotland) with Naoise, son of Usna, to escape the wrath of the King of Ireland, Conchobhar Mac Nessa, to whom Deirdre had been betrothed. They are said to have hidden in the Alder woods of Glen Etive, contributing in part to the themes of hiding and secrecy connected with Alder in Celtic lore.

A green dye can be derived from the flowers and this was used to colour and camouflage the garments of outlaws such as Robin Hood, as well as the clothes of faeries, concealing them from human eyes.

The wood from the Alder is oily and water resistant, turning hard when under water and so survives being submerged well. Consequently it was often used for the construction of buckets, water pipes, the foundations for bridges and other construction in wet conditions. Parts of Venice in Italy are built on top of Alder piles that were driven in to the Venetian lagoon. In Scotland, crannochs (wooden strongholds built over the water of Scottish lochs) were often built on rafts or piles of Alder trunks.

Like the Birch tree, Alder is considered to be a 'pioneer' tree, as it is often the first to colonise wet and treeless ground or to heal landscapes disturbed by fire, flood, clear cuts, or storms. They also have a unique characteristic that greatly improves the soil around them over the course of their life. They form a symbiotic relationship with a particular type of soil bacteria that takes up residence in their roots, that have nitrogen fixing nodules in them. This bacteria enables the Alder to make better use of the nitrogen in the air, in return for which the Alder provides the soil bacteria with sugar. The Alder's deep root system also helps to increase stability in river banks and other damp areas where the tree thrives.

Gort

G is for Gort
(pronounced 'GOR-ht')

Gort is associated with Ivy. In Celtic mythology Ivy is often associated with prosperity and growth, and it is believed to be a bringer of good fortune, particularly to women. Allowing it to grow up the outside walls of your home was thought to protect inhabitants from magic and curses. However, if it should die or fall down then misfortune would befall those who lived there.

Ivy represented peace to the Druids, who often related the Ivy to peace because of its ability to bind different plants together. It was frequently carried by young women for good luck and fertility, and today Ivy is often used at weddings, where it is seen to symbolise fidelity. The faeries are reputed to love Ivy as, along with Heather, is said not to grow in the faerie realm, accounting for why they like it so much.

H is for Huath
(pronounced 'HOO-er')

Huath is associated with Hawthorn. In Celtic mythology the thorns of the Hawthorn are often associated with cleansing, protection and defence.

Often called the Faerie Tree for it is said to guard the entrance to the faerie realm. The Scottish mystic and poet, Thomas the Rhymer, was said to have met the Faerie Queen under a Hawthorn tree. Having accompanied her into the faerie realm, he returned to find that he had been absent for seven years.

In Celtic mythology the Hawthorn was one of the most likely trees to be inhabited by faeries, and it was said that Hawthorn trees could not be cut down or damaged in any way without incurring the often fatal wrath of their supernatural guardians. In Celtic mythology faeries were not friendly little creatures that lived at the bottom of your garden, but were feared and respected, and tales of kidnapping and curses abound, so the Hawthorn was usually treated with care and respect.

I is for Iogh
(pronounced 'Yoo')

Iogh is associated with Yew. The Yew tree has come to symbolise death and resurrection in Celtic culture, perhaps because drooping branches of old Yew trees can root and form new trunks where they touch the ground, or because of their unusual growth pattern, in which new growth forms inside the old. Alternatively it might be because the Yew has no medicinal value at all, and almost all parts of it are toxic to humans and animals. However, Yew trees themselves are capable of living thousands of years and aged ones are often found in churchyards or in places that had pre-Christian spiritual significance. The Fortingall Yew in Perthshire is thought to be between 2,000 and 3,000 years old.

The Yew produces a very hard, close-grained wood that has commonly been used in furniture making, but is perhaps best known as the material from which English longbows were made.

L is for Luis
(pronounced 'LOO-sh')

Luis is associated with Rowan. The Rowan (also known as the Mountain Ash) is often associated with humanity, perseverance and life, as well as insight, blessings and protection against enchantments and magic. Celtic druids believed that women were forged from the Rowan tree (as men were forged from the Ash tree) and so the Rowan symbolises the fragility of life, motherhood, birth, and survival.

Rowan trees are not tall and therefore do not often grow in amongst taller trees, so are more commonly found growing singly. However, they can grow in shallow soil and at high altitude, making them common in the Scottish Highlands, often at altitudes where few other trees will grow. As the Celts believed that the veil between the heavens and the mortal world was thinnest on top of mountains where the land was closest to Heaven, this is perhaps why the Rowan has a special spiritual significance in Celtic mythology.

Muín

M is for Muin
(pronounced 'MOO-n')

Muin is commonly associated with the Vine, but also with the Bramble. Muin is a symbol of inward journeys and life lessons learned.

There is disagreement about whether Muin should be associated with the Vine, which although featured in Bronze Age art, isn't native, arriving in Britain when the Romans introduced wine 2000 years ago. The Bramble on the other hand is native to the cooler climate of Northern Europe and shares the winding characteristics and bares fruit like the Vine. In Gaelic the Bramble is known as Dris-Muine, which means 'Prickle Thorn', further supporting this theory.

This is why the Ogham Muin can represent either the Vine or the Bramble.

The Vine is a symbol of both happiness and wrath and is connected to prophecy and truthful speaking, perhaps because of the behaviours of those under the influence of fermented grapes used to make wine.

The Bramble is most commonly associated with the Devil and it was said that the Celts didn't eat Blackberries as the Devil had spat on them. The association with Satan is also present in Christian mythology, where it was said that when Satan was banished from the Kingdom of Heaven, he fell into a patch of brambles and cursed them as they pierced him. Goats are one of the few animals that eat brambles, and they are traditionally associated with Satan in Christianity, perhaps adding to the negative associations of the Devil with Brambles.

N is for Nuin
(pronounced 'NOO-n')

Nuin is associated with the Ash tree. The Ash tree has long been a symbol of wisdom, knowledge, and divination. Celtic druids also believed that men were forged from the Ash tree (and women from the Rowan) perhaps contributing to its association with masculinity, strength and rebirth.

In a number of legends, the Ash is connected to the Gods, and considered sacred. In Norse legend, Yggdrasil, the World Tree, is considered to be an Ash tree with its root reaching far down into the Underworld, its trunk reaching up into the Heavens, and its branches spreading out across all the countries on Earth. The Norse God Odin hung from Yggdrasil for nine days and was rewarded with insight and wisdom.

Ash has historically been seen as having healing and protective properties. In British folklore, newborn babies were often given a spoonful of Ash sap, whilst placing Ash berries in a cradle was thought to protect the child from being taken away as a changeling by mischievous faeries.

Most recently, Ash wood was used to make stagecoach axles as it was said to bear more weight than any other wood. Further back in history, spear shafts were often made of Ash, as were bows when Yew was not available.

The surname, Asher, is believed to be an English and Germanic occupational surname for an Ash maker, derived from the Middle English surname 'Aschere' or from German 'Äscher' (Ashman). In Old English it was used to mean someone who lived by an Ash tree or Ash grove. It has also been suggested that it was derived from a Viking term for spear maker. The Old Norse for an Ash tree was 'Askr' and for a spear was 'Atgeir' so this may be accurate.

Onn

O is for Onn
(pronounced 'OH-n')

Onn is associated with Gorse. In Celtic mythology Gorse (also known as Furze) was thought to provide protection against misfortune (and spiteful faeries - see below) and was also associated with resilience and optimism, as well as with the Sun, light, and fire. Gorse seeks sunshine and warmth and is quick to sprout new shoots. To this day, it is often cleared using a controlled burn to allow new gorse to come through.

In folklore there was a belief that protection from spiteful faeries could be achieved by completely barricading the space around your bed with Gorse branches!

Gorse wood burns at a high temperature with a fierce flame, similar to charcoal, and for this reason it was often used as a fuel. The flowers of the Gorse are bright yellow and can be used as a yellow dye for clothes. The Gorse generally flowers from January to June, although it can flower sporadically throughout the year.

Peith

P is for Peith
(pronounced 'Payh fhog')

Peith is associated with Downy Birch. As previously mentioned when describing Beith, in Celtic mythology Birch was traditionally associated with birth, love and purity. Birch was often placed over cradles to keep the young safe from evil spirits, and bundles of birch twigs were used to drive out the spirits of the old year.

Downy Birch is more upright than Silver Birch and the bark is browner in colour with more obvious horizontal grooves. It lacks the papery quality of the Silver Birch. Silver Birch has hairless and warty shoots whereas Downy Birch shoots are covered in small, downy hairs.

The range of Downy Birch is more Northerly and Westerly than Silver Birch, and it can grow at higher elevations. It can grow further North than any other broadleaf species. In the Spring, the sap from the Downy Birch can be used to make refreshing drinks including wines and ales.

Ruis

R is for Ruis
(pronounced 'Roosh')

Ruis is associated with Elder. Elder is often seen as representing endings, transitions, and maturity in terms of the the awareness that comes with experience.

In both Celtic and wider British folklore, Elder is said to provide protection against witches, malevolent faeries and the Devil. It was thought that if you burned the wood from the Elder, you would see the Devil, but if you planted Elder by your house it would keep the Devil away. Traditionally, it was said that the best protection for a home was obtained by having a Rowan tree by the front door and an Elder tree by the back door.

Elder wood is hard and off-white. The mature wood is good for whittling and carving, while smaller stems can be hollowed out to make craft items such as beads or musical instruments. It is said that the faery folk love music and merrymaking, and most of all they like the music from instruments made of Elder wood. Elder foliage was once used to keep flies away and branches were often hung around dairies in the belief that it would stop the milk from 'turning'. The flowers can be used to make wine, cordial or tea.

The Elder is not a common tree in Scotland, but many parts of the tree were historically used for dying in the Harris Tweed industry. Blue and purple dyes were obtained from the berries, yellow and green dyes from the leaves, and grey and black dyes from the bark.

S is for Suil
(pronounced 'Sool')

Suil is associated with Willow. In Celtic culture and lore, the Willow was associated with knowledge, optimism, adaptability and spiritual growth. The ease with which a new tree can be grown merely by pushing a healthy branch cutting into the soil has come to symbolise renewal, growth, vitality and immortality in other parts of the world.

Willow trees were an important part of Celtic mythology, and were thought of as sacred because they grow mostly on riverbanks and on the sides of lochs, both of which held special spiritual significance. Borders were important in Celtic culture, with the Rowan the most sacred for bordering the Earth and the Heavens, and Willow commonly growing on the border between land and water.

Whilst in many cultures, the Willow has been associated with sadness and mourning, this was not the case in Celtic culture where Willow was known for its ability to relocate after being uprooted, either by nature or by man. Much like the Alder, Willows are pioneer trees and they spread roots that help to stop soil erosion along banks in their natural, watery habitats.

Willow has been harvested for wicker work and baskets, small coracles, and even bee hives were constructed with this bendable, flexible wood. Most famously they are used in the construction of cricket bats and stumps. In the Nineteenth Century, scientists discovered that the Willow contains salicylic acid, which is similar to the active ingredient in Aspirin.

T is for Teine
(pronounced 'TEEN-uh')

Teine is associated with Holly. As an evergreen, Holly was connected with immortality, and a symbol of fertility and regeneration. Felling an entire Holly tree was said to have brought bad luck. However, the use of sprigs for decoration has always been allowed, and Holly has variously been brought into the house to protect the home from malevolent faeries or to allow faeries to shelter in the home without friction between them and the human occupants. Holly trees were also said to protect dwellings from lightening strikes if planted close to the home.

In folklore, the Holly was the King of the Woods for half the year, ruling from the Summer Solstice to the Winter Solstice, at which time Holly was defeated by the Oak King who ruled until the Summer Solstice again. In this way Holly was seen as the rival of Oak for the favour of the Lady of the Woods, Birch, who switched her allegiance from Oak to Holly and then back again.

Whilst it is now rare to see fully grown Holly trees, and more common to find it in hedges or as part of Oak or Beech woodland, large pieces of Holly wood have been used in furniture making and smaller pieces being used to make walking sticks. Holly wood is very heavy and hard, though fine grained, and is one of the whitest of all types of wood.

U is for Ur
(pronounced 'OohS')

Ur is associated with Heather. Heather symbolises luck, healing, passion and generosity, with flowers that are full of nectar and so attractive to bees, which are themselves seen as messengers between the spirit world and the mortal realm. In Scotland it competes with the Thistle to be the most iconic plant, where it is often seen as the Highland equivalent of the four-leafed Clover, especially white Heather. However, it is sometimes considered unlucky if brought indoors, though it could be used in this manner as a protection against witches.

It has been said that the faerie folk live in the Heather bells and that honey made from Heather is their favourite food. Heather, like Ivy is said not to grow in the faerie realm accounting for why they like it so much.